T0317790

Waterscapes

contemporary landscaping

The Deutsche Nationalbibliothek lists this publication in the Deutsche Nationalbibliografie; detailed bibliographical data are available on the internet at http://dnb.d-nb.de.

ISBN 978-3-03768-074-2
© 2011 by Braun Publishing AG
www.braun-publishing.ch

The work is copyright protected. Any use outside of the close boundaries of the copyright law, which has not been granted permission by the publisher, is unauthorized and liable for prosecution. This especially applies to duplications, translations, microfilming, and any saving or processing in electronic systems.

1st edition 2011

Project coordination: Editorial office van Uffelen
Editorial staff: Lisa Rogers, Chris van Uffelen
Translation preface: Geoffrey Steinherz
Graphic concept: Manuela Roth, Berlin
Layout: Theresa Beckenbauer, Sara Dame

All of the information in this volume has been compiled to the best of the editor's knowledge. It is based on the information provided to the publisher by the designers' offices and excludes any liability. The publisher assumes no responsibility for its accuracy or completeness as well as copyright discrepancies and refers to the specified sources (designers offices). All rights to the photographs are property of the photographer (please refer to the picture credits).

Chris van Uffelen

Waterscapes

contemporary landscaping

BRAUN

Content

Preface

Hydraulic engineering is one of the oldest activities of urban culture. Before the initial phase of the advanced cultures (coinciding with the development of writing in about 3000 B.C.) waterworks, consisting of drainage channels with inlet and outlet pipes became the precondition for agriculture, which in turn provided the conditions necessary for the emergence of urban cultural structures. The Codex Hammurabi, named after the king of the same name (1700 B.C.), passed down knowledge of the maintenance of irrigation systems, and the terraces of the so-called "hanging gardens" of Semiramis (about 600 B.C.) were certainly irrigated artificially.

Hydraulic engineering originally meant a system for hoisting water, which later included guiding it through a conduit system. The Dutch, who for hundreds of years have practiced landscape conservation with the aid of polders, brooks, locks and pumps in order to create useful land, have the longest tradition of extensive experience in dealing with water. Evidence from Nero's palace, the Domus Aurea shows that hydraulic engineering began in ancient times with water wheels and the Archimedean screw pump, also used at the time for the operation of trick fountains, wells and cascades. At the very latest this could be called the beginning of the history of "waterscaping", or landscape architecture with water. The Roman facilities, which fell into ruins after the collapse of the Empire, have been reconstructed in modern times. Various popes had the great "waterways" from the antique period, reconstructed and in place of the original Asclepeion, commissioned the construction of huge fountains as a demonstration of their power. For instance, the 50 meter wide Fontana de Trevi was built under Clemens XII from 1732 to 1762 according to a design by Nicola Salvi at the termination of the Aqua Virgo aqueduct. In the modern period many elaborate trick fountains were built in parks, belonging to the nobility, like the Bergpark at Schloss Wilhelmshöhe in Kassel (built by Giovanni Francesco Guerniero, expanded in 1785 by Heinrich Christoph Jussow). The brooks, cascades, aqueduct, waterfalls and the 52-meter-high shooting fountains all work without resorting to water hoisting, relying entirely on natural gradients and a 40,000-cubic-meter capacity reservoir. Today the technical effort of trick fountains is much easier to operate than was the case in the past. In contrast, the actual artistic task has remained constant: the water should be a source of joy for the visitors and liven up the landscape. But waterscapes are more than just trick fountains. As an aesthetic or contemplative moment in the design of the environment, the calm surface of a pool, which serves as a mirror for the surroundings or the sky, is also a waterscape. The construction of embankments and the seemingly inconspicuous renaturalization of bodies of water also belong to the disciplines of the genre.

This volume presents the most diverse forms of water that appears in landscape architecture. In addition to large landscape designs there are waterfalls, and fountains emerging from the pavement, without any trace of green, water surfaces with rigorous contours, rainwater diverted from the roof and even planned puddles. It shows how water caresses, contradicts or continues the architecture, how it creates calm or excitement, attracting the attention of the visitors or guiding them along their way. Water – with some of these buildings it can be a very small amount – is one of the most decisive elements of these designs.

Jacob Isaacksz. van Ruisdael: Mill at Wijk at Duurstede, 1670 (Detail).

Lake Michelle

Cape Town, South Africa
Landscape Design: Tanya de Villiers of CNdV Africa
Completion: 2007
Client: Plan Trust
Photos: Christof Heierli

Lake Michelle is an environmentally sensitive estate, nestled around a 300,000 square meter saline lake in Noordhoek. The landscape architect built in 70,000 square meter of ponds and reed beds, which increased property values whilst aerating and cleaning the lake water. The careful design of roads, bridges, ponds, boardwalks, lighting, signage and green space creates a unique environment. Reed beds, sandy beaches and islands act as bird sanctuaries. The site was covered in non-indigenous species but 50,000 remaining indigenous plants were rescued. This ensures sustainability and links the site with adjacent natural areas.

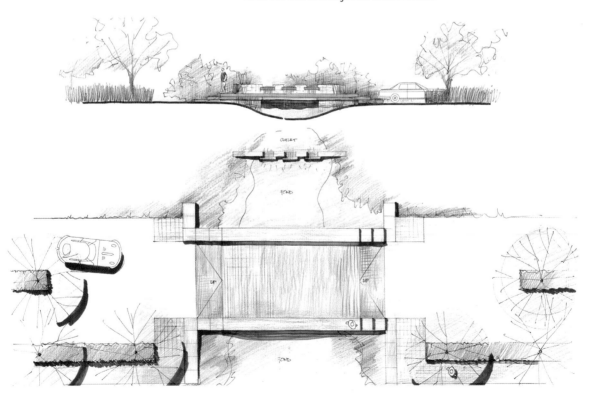

Left: Entrance bridge and circulation pond.
Right: Concept plan for a bridge crossing.

Top: The site is entered across a pond which introduces the water theme.
Bottom: Jetties provide access to the lake for water sport.
Right: Hardwood, indigenous grass and other permeable surfaces.

Lite-On Headquarters

Taipei, Taiwan
Landscape Design: SWA Group
Architecture: Innerscapes Designs
Completion: 2003
Client: Artech-Inc.
Photos: Tom Fox

SWA provided landscape design for the Lite-On Electronic Headquarters in Taipei, Taiwan. The total area for the site is 10,152 square meters. There is a 25-story tower, which sits on the top of a large podium, sloping towards the river. The design emphasizes the view towards the city and river from the podium garden. Additionally, the focus of the design is to unify the sloped podium garden and the courtyards below with the landscape area outside the building. The owner had a vision of sustainability before the current LEED accreditation became a popular project goal and the landscape became a green roof – the first of its kind to be envisioned and built by a private developer in Taipei.

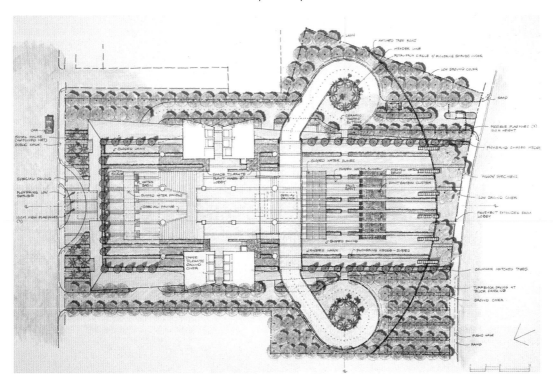

Left: Detail of waterfall from the five roof terrace canals above.
Right: Site masterplan.

Top: Sloped roof terrace garden at drop-off area.
Bottom: One of the five roof terrace canals.
Right: Sunken court garden for the food and conference area.

Hong Kong Wetland Park

Hong Kong, China
Landscape Design: Urbis Limited
Architecture: Architectural Services Department
Completion: 2005
Client: Agriculture, Fisheries & Conservation Department
Photos: Courtesy of the architects

The Hong Kong Wetland Park is regarded as a prime example of sound environmental practices and sustainable development. Unique to Hong Kong, the park seeks to cater equally for the functions of conservation, tourism, education and recreation. The structures of its buildings were purposely designed with landscape roofs and timber shades. The Visitor Center consists of exhibition galleries, office, cafe, souvenir shop, play area and toilets. The Wetland Discovery Center and three bird hides are located in the recreated wetland habitats of the external area, together with fixed and floating boardwalk paths, which all serve unique functions in supporting the aim of wetland conservation.

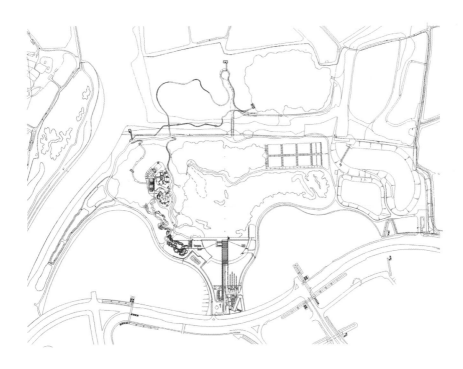

Left: Entrance plaza leads to lawn roofed Visitor Center.
Right: Site plan.

Top: Reflection of the Visitor Center at the lake.
Bottom: Fair face concrete walls sitting quietly over the lake.
Right: Discovery Center over the Lily pond.

Bassil Mountain Escape

Faqra, Lebanon
Landscape Design: Vladimir Djurovic Landscape Architecture
Architecture: Kamal Homsi
Completion: 2003
Client: Jimmy Bassil
Photos: Geraldine Bruneel

The challenge of this project was to provide space to accommodate various functions in an extremely narrow site. The garden was built almost entirely on the construction setback of 4.5 meter around the house. The program consists of multiple sitting areas, a water mirror with a cantilevered Jacuzzi, underneath which an outdoor bar area is sheltered, a swimming pool, a terrace with a long linear bench, and a fireplace and BBQ area. The negative-edge Jacuzzi and swimming pool frame the breathtaking view. Floating stepping-stones lead guests down to the bar area, which consists of solid stone and red cedar wood. The long linear bench acts as a safety balustrade and rest area for large gatherings.

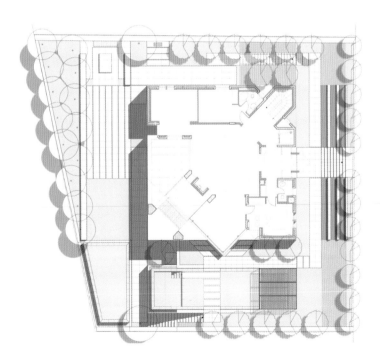

Left: Water mirror reflecting the residence, bridging the small site with panoramic views.
Right: Site plan.

Top: A serene contemplative water mirror, extending the realms of the tight space.
Bottom: Cantilevered jacuzzi shading lower bar area.
Right: View from inside out with water and panoramic.

Xilinx Colorado Corporate Campus

Longmont, CO, USA
Landscape Design: Dtj Design
Architecture: Dtj Design – Architecture
Completion: 2002
Client: Xilinx
Photos: Robb Williamson, Denver

Dtj provided the masterplan, landscape architecture, and architecture for this project. The design takes advantage of existing wetlands, trees, creeks and mountain views and the final design minimized the impact on those amenities. Landscape materials were used to complement the buildings. Stone, water and plants were incorporated into the construction for a seamless indoor/outdoor relationship, anchoring the building to its site. The landscape includes private outdoor rooms, work spaces, meeting areas and retreats. The sustainable design employs concepts such as energy conservation, use of 'green' products, native materials, and water/storm water management measures.

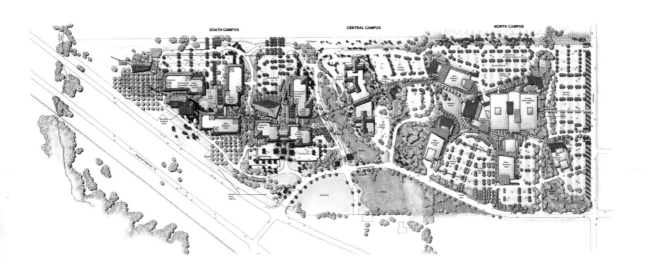

Left: Waterfall below bridge to retreat building.
Right: Overall masterplan.

Top: Winter garden.
Bottom: Commuter parking.
Right: Created mountain stream.

Urban Dock LaLaport Toyosu

Tokyo, Japan
Landscape Design: Earthscape
Architecture: Laguarda.Low Architects
Completion: 2006
Client: Mitsui Fudosan Group Ltd. / Ishikawajima-Harima Heavy Industries Company
Photos: Koji Okumura / Forward Stroke, Japan

LaLaport is a renowned shopping mall in Japan, offering sightseeing, entertainment and shopping. It is located in the center of Toyosu in Koto district, Tokyo on an area of 6.7 hectare. Facing the Harumi Canal it includes many remains of the shipbuilding industry. Earthscape was commissioned to develop this site into a comprehensive commercial area across two blocks. The designers focused on the conservation of the ancient ruins and a dynamic streetscape. The area around the old dock was renovated into an entertainment ground. Some remains such as cranes and propellers were carefully preserved to create an area filled with memories and fun. A waterfront promenade was also included where people can go for pleasant walks.

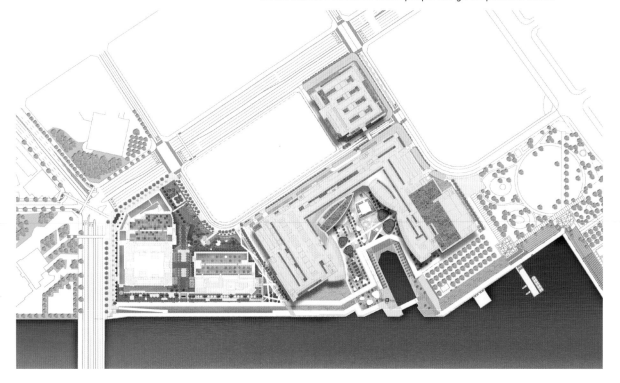

Left: Place.
Right: Site plan.

Top: Twilight.
Bottom: Path in bassin.
Right: Urban dock.

Casa Cor 2006

Sao Paulo, Brazil
Landscape Design: Marcelo Novaes Paysagismo LDTA.
Completion: 2006
Client: Casa Cor
Photos: Courtesy of the architects

The "Casa Cor" exhibition is one of the most anticipated architecture, decoration and landscaping events in South America. The most prominent architects and landscape artists of the region gather here to show their creations. This garden was situated in an outdoor salon of the Jockey Club. Equipped with a lounge, betting area and a bar it is situated right in front of the horse tracks, allowing the spectators to comfortably enjoy the races. One of the most important aspects of the design is the use of noble and natural materials to make it pleasant, functional and esthetically attractive. The elements water and fire additionally create a very rich and pleasurable ambience.

Left: Fountain with the Buxus sempervirens and the Dracaena arborea.
Right: Fountain overlooking the fireplace.

Top: *Fountain in front of the salon compliments the entryway of the salon.*
Bottom: *Fountain with the Buxus sempervirens and the Dracaena arborea.*
Right: *Black granite path, the fountain leading up to the fireplace, the flame is reflected in the water.*

Acuario Fluvial EXPO Zaragoza

Zaragoza, Spain
Landscape Design: Álvaro Planchuelo
Architecture: Álvaro Planchuelo
Completion: 2008
Client: Sociedad EXPO Zaragoza 2008
Photos: Alberto Cubas, Ricardo Santonja

Water and its sustainable use in developing the banks of the River Ebro served as the central theme of the Expo 2008 in Zaragoza. The Acuario Fluvial, "Pavilion of the Rivers", presents the waterscapes of great rivers, namely the Nile, Amazon, Mekong, Darling and Ebro, as well as the River of the World, representing the prehistoric Ocean. The individual aquaria spaces are interconnected by walkways across a huge central tank. The façades are encased in various materials. Museography was made by Coutant Aquariums.

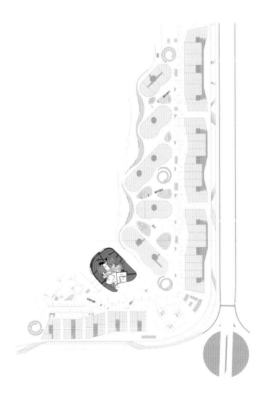

Left: Terrace, "the frozen lake".
Right: Site plan.

Top: West elevation, "the mountain glaciers, the arid land, rock and water landscapes".
Bottom: Terrace, view of the "frozen lake" from the "arid land".
Right: Aquarium entrance, "the mountain glaciers".

Bundesplatz Swiss Federal Piazza

Berne, Switzerland
Landscape Design: Stauffenegger + Stutz with Stephan Mundwiler
Completion: 2004
Client: City of Berne, Swiss Government
Photos: Ruedi Walti

This is the most famous square in Switzerland. Its rectangular 60x30 meter natural stone feature precisely bases on the geometry of the parliament building. The large stone slabs of strongly textured Gneiss from the Vals region are positioned symmetrical, resulting in large-scale ornaments. The stone surface is crossed by a slightly curved band of light, which illustrates the movement of people from the Bärenplatz in the direction of the Bundes-haus. A fountain, with nozzles integrated into the floor, allows the square to appear as a three dimensional element. In 2006 the project won the Honor Award for Urban Design from the American Institute of Architects (AIA).

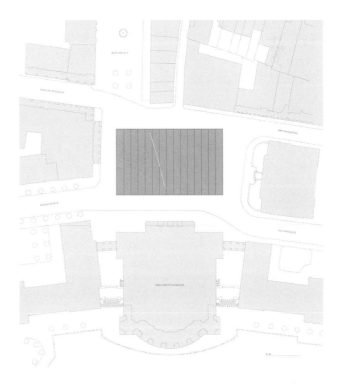

Left: Fountains view by night.
Right: Site plan.

Top: Overall view.
Bottom: Fountains at twilight.
Right: Lighted place.

Stanley Park Salmon Stream

Vancouver, Canada
Landscape Design: PWL Landscape Architects
Completion: 2001
Client: Vancouver Board of Parks and Recreation & Vancouver Aquarium Marine Science Centre
Photos: Alex Piro, PWL

Set within Vancouver's historic 405 hectare Stanley Park, the Stanley Park Salmon Stream is a human-created stream draining to the adjacent Coal Harbour and successfully supporting returning salmon populations. The primary project goals were to utilize waste salt water from the Vancouver Aquarium, to address the urgent issue of salmon habitat loss in urban areas, and to reclaim hardscape areas. The stream replaces approximately one hectare of paved parking lot and consists of an upper freshwater portion and a lower salt water portion, separated by a weir. A series of interpretive panels illustrate the importance of stream conservation and restoration for dwindling salmon and steelhead populations.

Left: Jump cascades are designed for specific species of salmon.
Right: New salmon stream introduced into Stanley Park.

Top: Resting pool with lookout.
Bottom: Large woody debris and vegetative cover enhance salmon habitat.
Right: Variety in stream depth, width, and cover mimic a natural stream.

Remanso de las Condes

Santiago, Chile
Landscape Design: Arqui-K Arquitectura + Paisaje
Architecture: Karla Aliaga, Carol Litin, Omar Garrido
Completion: 2008
Client: Inmobiliaria DICAL
Photos: Italo Arriaza

The focus of this proposal was to incorporate the local habitat into the design, using the native species, Acacia caven and different ground textures. The set finishes off at one of the model homes of the condominium, within which the outside lines are continued, adding pure and orthogonal guidelines to model the landscape. Horizontal and vertical elements are incorporated (water mirror and bamboo), which augment the angular character of the house architecture. In the garden of the house, mosses and creeping plants were used to cover the natural and modeled slopes, unifying the whole set with ornamental trees like cyprus gras (Cyperus alternifolius), Japanese maple (Acer palmatum) and crepe flower (Lagestroemia indica).

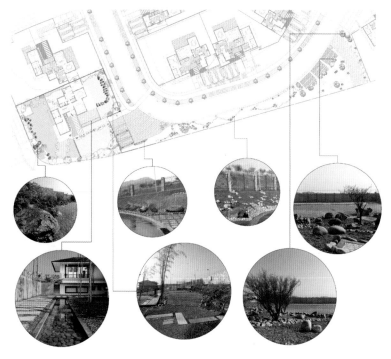

Left: Water mirror at entrance.
Right: Situation plan.

Top: Angular shapes and variuos textures give sobriety to the set. Distinctly angular design imprints the orthogonal character of the garden.
Bottom: View of perimeter flowerbed.
Right: Gray gravel island and sandstone footpath.

Water Treatment Park Het Lankheet

Haaksbergen, The Netherlands
Landscape Design: Strootman Landscape Architects,
Amsterdam
Completion: 2008
Client: Lankheet bv
Photos: Harry Cock, Assen (52, 55), Strootman Landscape
Architects, Amsterdam (54)

The design transforms "Het Lankheet" country estate into a spectacular water garden, also revealing the logic of the water purification system. The several parts of the water machine are connected by water and a sinuous dyke, which acts as both the spatial backbone and a lookout point. New forests are being planted to evoke a fairy-tale atmosphere, while parts of the existing forest are being transformed into a woodland garden. The new extensive water-channel system creates an almost meditative environment. The visitor is guided through the complex on the serpentine dyke that weaves its way through the misty channels, with monumental woodland as a permanent backdrop.

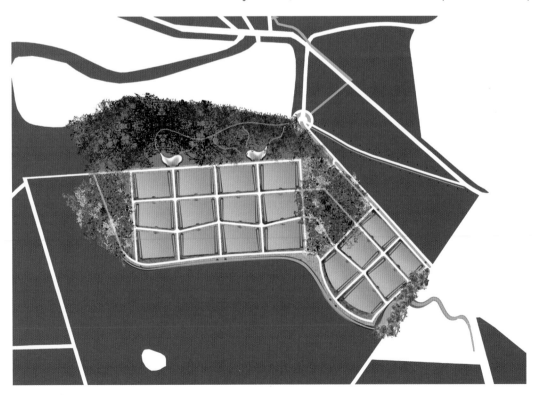

Left: Panorama dyke.
Right: Plan of Water Treatment Park.

Top: Vistor in filtrations fields.
Bottom: Woodlands with pond.
Right: Filtration fields with reed.

Ridge and Valley

Pennsylvania, PA, USA
Landscape Design: Stacy Levy
Architecture: Mtr Landscape Architects
Completion: 2009
Client: The Pennsylvania State University
Photos: Fredric Weber (56, 59), Stacy Levy (58)

The local Spring Creek Watershed of the Ridge and Valley region is recreated in a bluestone terrace, punctuated by three boulder 'ridges' that rise from the terrace and create seating walls. All of the local streams and waterways are depicted with runnels carved 0.63 centimeters deep into the stone. When it is dry, this terrace is a scale map of the geology and watershed of this area. But when it rains, the Visitors Pavilion roof drains onto the terrace and the rainfall flows across the carved waterways, creating a watershed in miniature. The artwork is both a place-making object and an engineering system; and it gives visitors a way to celebrate the hydrological cycle.

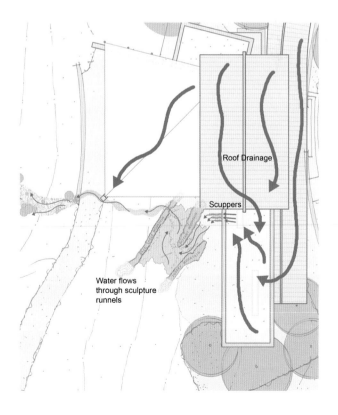

Left: Overall view.
Right: Ridge and valley plan.

Top: During a rainy day.
Bottom: After a rainstorm.
Right: Seating detail.

Freedom Park

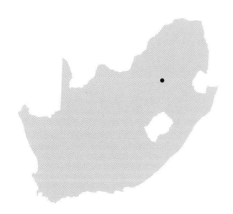

Tshwane, South Africa
Landscape Design: NLA Bagale GREENinc Momo
Joint Venture
Architecture: Office of Collaborative Architects
Completion: 2007
Client: Freedom Park Trust
Photos: Graham Young (60, 62), Tristan McLaren (63)

Freedom Park is a National Legacy project mandated by Nelson Mandela and envisioned to celebrate South Africa's rich heritage. Five key elements; //hapo, Isivivane, Sikumbuto, Moshate and Tiva form the basis of a narrative and are linked by a wheelchair friendly pathway system. These elements are contained within a Garden of Remembrance. Sikhumbuto is a memorial to those people who fell during the various conflicts that gave birth to a democratic South Africa. It is comprised of the Wall of Names, Sanctuary, Reeds, Gallery of Leaders and Moshate. The final phase will see the completion of Tiva and //hapo, an interpretive center and Pan-Africa archive.

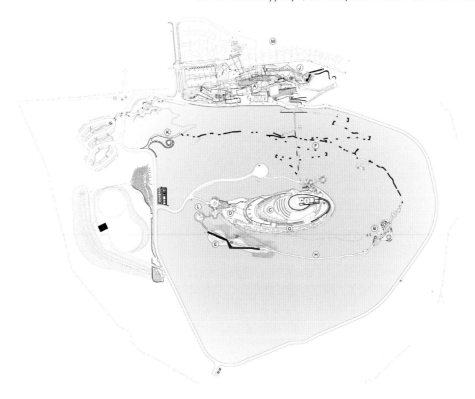

Left: Waterfall.
Right: Freedom Park Plan.

Top: Detail of waterfall.
Bottom: Bird's-eye view.
Right: Sanctuary Water Feature.

Zhengzhou University Campus Center

Zhengzhou City, China
Landscape Design: Beijing Turen Design Institution/
Turenscape
Architecture: Kongjian Yu, Shihong Ling, Jing Niu, Yang Pan
Completion: 2006
Client: Zhengzhou University
Photos: Courtesy of the architects

This new campus was designed to give an identity to this newly created university, which merged three older ones, and to act as a uniting force, binding the former, separate institutes together. This project is located in the center of the new campus right in front of the main class room building. It also acts as a separating and the uniting green between the living zones and the academic zone. The iconic landscape collects storm water from all over the campus, the vegetation consists of native plants that change through the seasons and need little maintenance. Various bridges are designed to allow people enter the landscape and the native plant sections. Platforms and seating places allow students to fully interact with nature.

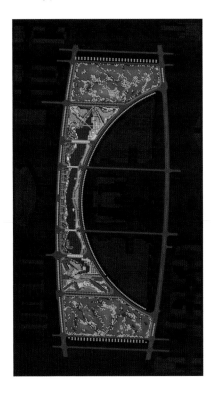

Left: Bridge and lake.
Right: Site plan.

Top: Walking through the nature.
Bottom: Path of black stones over water.
Right: Balk at the waterside.

Parc Central

Kirchberg, Luxembourg
Landscape Design: Latz + Partner with Latz Riehl Partner
Completion: 2006
Client: Ministère des Bâtiments Publics
Photos: Latz + Partner (68, 71), Michael Latz (70)

This project was an essential part of an ongoing town renewal venture, which started in the 1990s. The different areas of the city needed to be formed into a coherent, inhabitable and vibrant city space, accommodating the different areas of life; living, working, education and leisure. In this process, the shape of public open spaces is not so much the point, but rather the coherence of their structure. The characteristic town quarters are structured by avenues, squares, gardens and parks along an old Roman road. The park, with a specific design language and a "European Arboretum", directly connects to the re-structured city streets and the city boulevard using the image of local old vineyard walls.

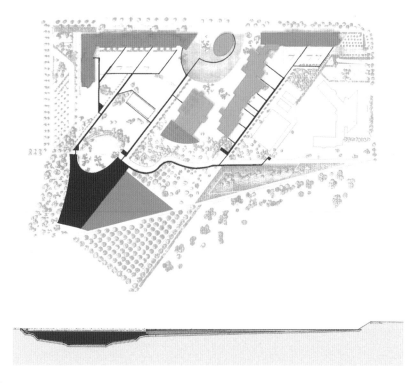

Left: Water falling from above.
Right: Site plan and section.

Top: Bird's-eye view.
Bottom: Fountains.
Right: Lakeside terrace.

Place des Nations

Geneva, Switzerland
Landscape Design: Christian Drevet Architecture
Architecture: Christian Drevet Architecture with Arlette Ortis
Completion: 2007
Client: City of Geneva
Photos: Alain Grandchamp, City of Geneva

The outstanding new features of this square include its pavement design, fountain and lighting. Pavement stones made of granite from 20 countries in all colors of the rainbow contrast with the 'neutral' tone of the concrete – the construction material traditionally used in Geneva. The fountain without a basin consists of seven lines of 12 jets of water with variable spray patterns. The design of the central area was made to resemble a theater, resulting in a topologic organization with various sections: the stage is represented by the central square, the wings by its sides, while the setting is the Palais des Nations with its flags, and the 'foyer' is the garden of the Place des Nations.

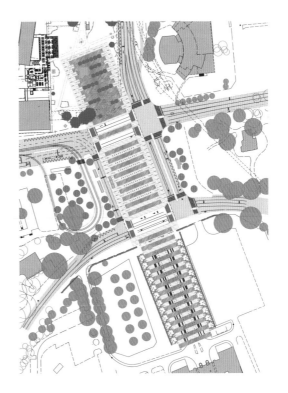

Left: Broken chair.
Right: Masterplan.

Top: Wings.
Bottom: Water jets.
Right: View at night.

Opus 22

Genessee, CO, USA
Landscape Design: Marpa Design Studio
Architecture: Sears Barrett Architects
Completion: 2001
Client: James Williams
Photos: Martin Mosko

Located in the Rocky Mountains of Colorado, this private garden has won numerous state and national awards. Its rivers and waterfalls flow down to what seems to be a mountain lake, while giant boulders create their own inspiring view. The vanishing edge of the small upper pool is echoed in the much larger swimming pool, drawing the eye to the magnificent view beyond. A special feature is a water slide that runs through the heart of the mountain. The landscape connects the home to its environment through the use of natural stone, native plants, and giant trees.

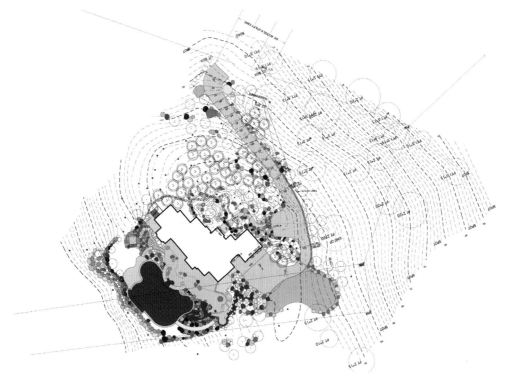

Left: Waterfall.
Right: Pool panorama.

Top: View from balcony.
Bottom: Small waterfall.
Right: Pool and house.

Holstebro Storaa Stream

Holstebro, Denmark
Landscape Design: OKRA landschapsarchitecten bv
Completion: 2006
Client: Holstebro City Council
Photos: OKRA

The public spaces around different cultural buildings provide new élan to the city by transforming them into an outdoor stage. 'Foldings' are creating a continuous space of paths, small spots and places to sit. A bridge takes a central position, tying the folded urban realm of both riverbanks together, being a place where people can pass or citizens can stay and watch the scenery. On the other side the former parking space in the south is transformed into a stage, having a large water feature and long stairs. The film of water on a paved area is sometimes a fountain or a place for children to play with, sometimes just an object to watch from the adjacent stairs.

Left: Steps and water.
Right: Site plan.

Top: Bassin as counterpart of channel.
Bottom: Bridge crossing the river/channel.
Right: Playing with water.

Campeon

Neubiberg, Germany
Landscape Design: Rainer Schmidt Landschaftsarchitekten and GTL Landschaftsarchitekten
Architecture: TEC PCM, Maier Neuberger Architekten
Completion: 2006
Client: Mo To Projektmanagement GmbH
Photos: Raffaella Sirtoli

Water creates atmosphere – both visually and ecologically. The ring-shaped, 6.8-hectare Campeon pond not only attracts users during break time on a workday but also improves the microclimate and serves as a retention and seepage basin for the rainwater. The pond is fed by rainwater and snow. In order to keep water quality high, the water is changed completely once a year. Towards the Campeon grounds there are a waterside promenade and squares with stands of trees. Here the shore drops in the form of a steep grassy bank or a concrete edge down to the water. Like bastions, small squares push into the pond. A Corten steel water table and linear seating elements along the length of the pool invite visitors to linger near the water.

Left: Pond.
Right: Site plan.

Top: Different banks.
Bottom: Promenade.
Right: Water table.

Dragon Castle Park

Chen Du, China
Landscape Design: Palm Landscape Planning & Design
Institute, Palm Landscape Architecture Co. Ltd.
Architecture: Wenying Zhang, Wei He
Completion: 2007
Client: Chen Du Zhi Da Estate Co. Ltd.
Photos: Wenying Zhang

Dragon Castle Park belongs to the Dragon Castle No.1 project in Chen Du,
China. The western part of the site is rich with terrain elevation differences.
The masterplan took advantage of the height differences, designed great
waterscapes and setting out to establish leisure areas as far away as pos-
sible from the high-voltage towers. Dragon stone sculpture, the "L" shape
of the complex and the meandering stream are all linked to the main theme
of Dragon. As the greatest green site, this park focuses on providing open
space near people's homes to allow sports activities, gatherings and further
kinds of entertainment.

Left: Megalithic Dragon scultpure and fountain.
Right: Sketch of water feature.

Top: View of wood pavilion and waterfall.
Bottom: View of water feature.
Right: View of lake.

EhMaHo

Castle Pines, CO, USA
Landscape Design: Marpa Landscape Design Studio
Architecture: Semple/Brown Architects
Completion: 2008
Client: Jerry and Mary Kern
Photos: Martin Mosko

The house that previously stood here was oriented to a golf course and not to the gardens in the back. The architect Chris Davis created a new, very modern house which faces the garden superbly. The client asked Marpa to design an entry garden for the new house that was congruent with the new space as well as the existing gardens. This resulted in "EhMaHo". One descends three meters from the street level alongside a water wall to a stone bridge crossing the water toward the front door. The water has vanishing edges in all directions. Form-board concrete walls (four meters) create an outdoor room with the sky as a ceiling.

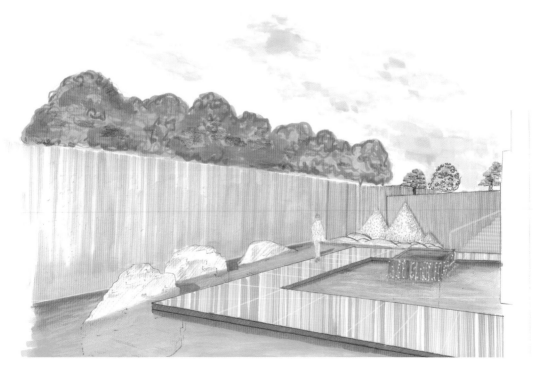

Left: View of house and water.
Right: Sketch.

Top: Form-board concrete and two sculptural gongs designed by Richard Lee.
Bottom: Path of stone over the water.
Right: View over water, garden and a water wall animating the space with sound.

Katharina Sulzer-Platz

Winterthur, Switzerland
Landscape Design: vetschpartner Landschaftsarchitekten AG Zurich
Completion: 2004
Client: Sulzer Immobilien
Photos: Ralph Feiner

This space impresses with its dimensions, the defining sequence of façades of the industrial and residential architecture and the enormous contrast between the sweep of open landscape and the surrounding, built-up density. The programmatic concept rests on a visually homogeneous, but changeable surface. The finishes incorporate refined materials from the former factory. The water represents visual breadth, a puddle, spill, plaything, a fleeting element and medium for altering the surface.

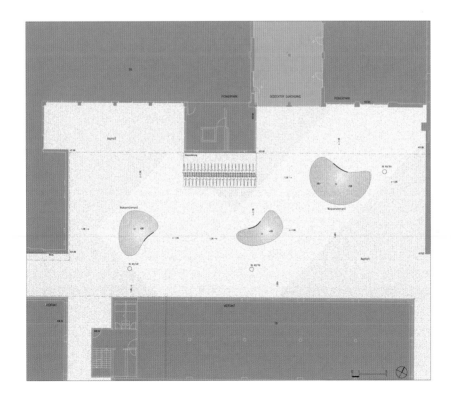

Left: Night view.
Right: Plan courtyard.

Top: Detail of puddle.
Bottom: Public open space with seating.
Right: Puddles.

Chelsea Courtyard

London, United Kingdom
Landscape Design: Charlotte Rowe Garden Design
Completion: 2010
Client: Private
Photos: Charlotte Rowe Garden Design/Light IQ (100, 102 a., 103), Charlotte Rowe Garden Design/Andrew Ewing (102 b.)

This tiny (40 square meter) courtyard is accessed and viewed both from the drawing room and the kitchen and is an integral part of this family house in London. The paving, steps and cladding for the benches is in the same pale cream limestone used throughout the ground floor of the house making the courtyard become a continuation of the interior space. The one meter long cantilevered bronze spout feeds water into the narrow rill which runs down the garden and is lit for dramatic effect at night. The horizontal slatted trellis in Western Red Cedar is down-lit, the bronze canopy over the fold back doors is under-lit with fibre optics creating a starry night effect. The planting is soft and gentle to counter contemporary style and the stone surfaces.

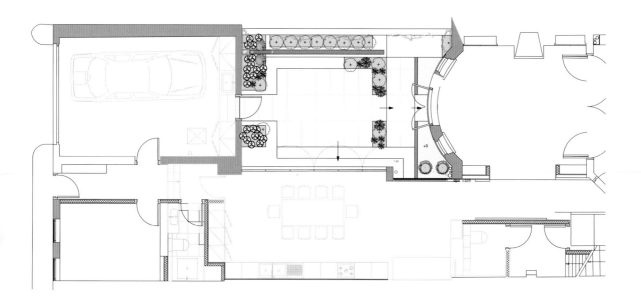

Left: Water flows into the rill bordered by soft planting.
Right: Ground floor plan showing garden layout.

Top: Cantilevered bronze water spout.
Bottom: The courtyard and kitchen are a unified space.
Right: Cantilevered bronze spout feeds water into long water rill.

Floating Islands of Sunflowers

Kiminomori New Town, Chiba Prefecture, Japan
Landscape Design: Ryumei Fujiki + Fujiki Studio, KOU::ARC
Architecture: Ryumei Fujiki + Fujiki Studio, KOU::ARC
Completion: 2002
Client: Art Front Gallery
Photos: Ryumei Fujiki

The objective of this project was to shorten the psychological distance between the community of Kiminomori and the golf course around which the town is situated, by sharing the scenery for one summer only with a group of sunflowers floating in the pond on the eighth hole of the Kiminomori Golf Club. The throng of sunflowers sways gently in the breeze on the pond and is reflected on the water's surface. This unrealistic scene was created based on the keyword of 'nature'. The feature included blue lighting that was lit during an evening music concert, sponsored by the Kiminomori Golf Club for local residents, the night flowers illuminated with a mystical blue light bloomed all around, creating a dramatic change from the scene portrayed during the day.

Left: View over waterscape.
Right: Detail of a base and site plan.

Top: Overview.
Bottom: Detail of the floating objects.
Right: View of the water and houses.

Stonehurst Mountain Estate

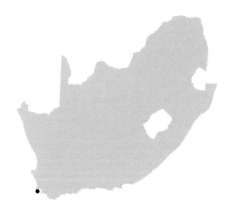

Tokai, South Africa
Landscape Design: Tanya de Villiers of CNdV Africa
Completion: 2007
Client: Mvelaprop
Photos: Christof Heirli

Stonehurst Mountain Estate is a residential development on a highly degraded site. Streams and wetlands, which were completely destroyed by previous developers, have been rehabilitated to form attractive riverine and wetland areas. Signage, detailing and road finishes were chosen to reflect the colors and textures of the mountain above the site. Plants from the mountain now inhabit these rehabilitated open spaces. Ponds and reed beds were created in order to cleanse rainwater-runoff from buildings.

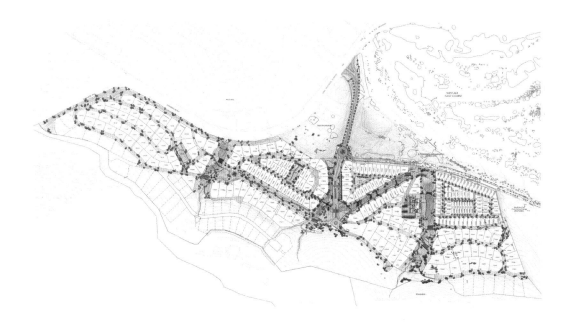

Left: Matching stone from the site was used to clad the waterfall, the source of the main water feature.
Right: Landscape masterplan.

Top: The entrance and water feature are lit at night.
Bottom: Reed beds and ponds were created to cleanse storm water off buildings.
Right: A linear water feature cascades down the center of the entrance road.

Estate Hageveld

Heemstede, The Netherlands
Landscape Design: Bureau Alle Hosper with De Stijlgroep
Architecture: Bureau Alle Hosper with MYJ groep
Artist: Hermine van der Does
Completion: 2007
Client: Hopman Interheem Groep
Photos: Pieter Kers, Amsterdam

In 2002 a plan was made to transform the Hageveld Estate into private housing and expand the space for school sporting activities. The landscape intervention enhances the green character of the estate and restores the heavily damaged planting on the west side of the estate with trees. The large pond was designed on top of a new underground car park. The entrance slope slits through the water and glass panels ensure that daylight can enter and the fountains produce bubbles just above water level. The Hageveld estate is reestablished as a complete unit. It is open to the public, offering the different types of users a peaceful, green, historic setting for a wide range of activities.

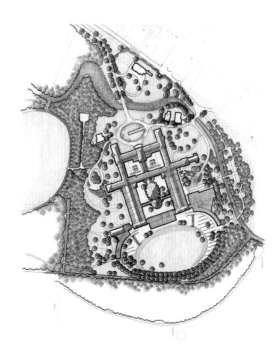

Left: Night view of glass panels with artwork.
Right: Plan of the estate grounds.

Top: Night view of pond from main building.
Bottom: Front entrance of the main building.
Right: View of pond from the west.

General Mills Corporate Campus

Golden Valley, MN, USA
Landscape Design: Oslund.and.assoc
Architecture: HGA
Completion: 2004
Client: General Mills
Photos: Heinrich Photography, Minnesota

General Mills Corporate Campus is a statement of 1950s modernism jux-taposed with a pastoral landscape. With the acquisition of the Pillsbury Corporation, the campus needed to expand substantially to accommodate two additional buildings. The landscape architect was required to create a setting with the illusion that the new buildings were floating within the landscape, touching a static plane of water. Formal site plantings directly adjacent to the buildings helped reinforce the architecture, while farther out an undulating natural landscape reinforces the attitude so complimen-tary to the site sculpture.

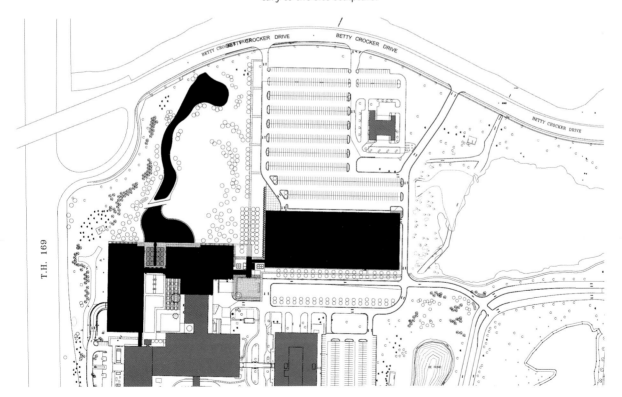

Left: The outdoor dining terrace, nestled between the new buildings, fronts on a new pond.
Right: Plan of the General Mills Campus.

Top: The new dining terrace serves as a popular lunchtime destination for General Mills employees.
Bottom: Fall on the dining terrace with views across the pond into the pastoral surroundings.
Right: Looking across the water feature and bridge towards the Borovsky sculpture.

Bao Yuan Garden

Hangzhou, China
Landscape Design: Palm Landscape Planning & Design Institute, Palm Landscape Architecture
Architecture: Wenying Zhang, Hualin Xu
Completion: 2008
Client: Hangzhou Yuhang Xincheng Estate
Photos: Wenying Zhang

The landscape design of Bao Yuan Garden is concerned with representing the spirit and ideology of the Chiang-Nan water country. Two ancient bridges were to be preserved, with the aim of symbolizing the process of urban development with its roots in village life. One of the bridges was built during Ming Dynasty, the other during Manchu Dynasty. Both bridges were reconstructed for this central garden, becoming symbols of development. Artist Han Meiling created the sculptures in the garden, which symbolize family fortune. Bao Yuan Garden beautifully combines adequately modern architecture with ancient elements and materials.

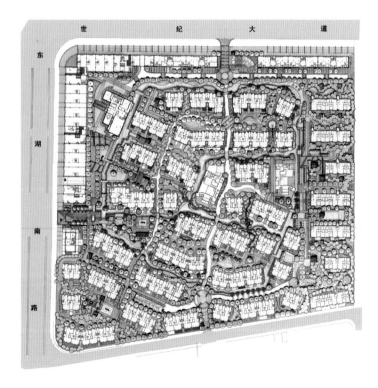

Left: Streamlet wandered around each building.
Right: Bao Yuan Garden masterplan.

Top: The dialogue between building, water and tree.
Bottom: Harmonious blend of bronze sculpture and vivacious waterscape.
Right: Remarkable waterscapes, the paving built with ancient brick, abstract Chinese characters pattern.

North Island

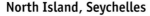

North Island, Seychelles
Landscape Design: Patrick Watson, Greg Wepene
Architecture: Silvio Resch, Lesley Carstens
Completion: 2003
Client: North Island
Photos: Chris van Uffelen (124, 126 b., 127),
Michael Poliza (126 a.)

North Island was planned as a "Noah's Ark project" and involved the restoration of an entire island from its damaged state brought on by commercial exploitation that began in 1826. The island had been used as a plantation for growing fruits and spices and, later, producing copra – oil pressed from coconut flesh. Cultivation and replanting of native plants as well as removal of alien species was a major part of the project. Several luxury villas handcrafted form local wood and stone were erected. The proceeds are used to bankroll the renaturalization project. The interplay of architecture, landscape architecture and interior design established a new style – the "Robinson Crusoe Haute Couture."

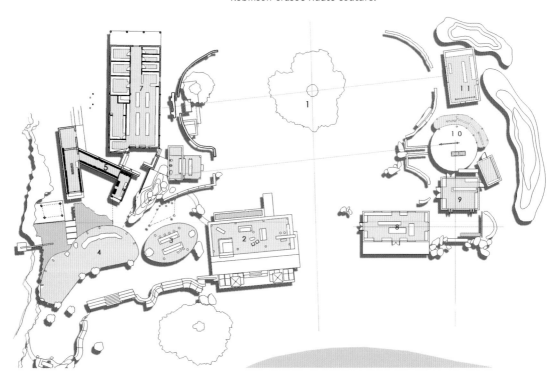

Left: Next to the restaurant.
Right: Site plan central court.

Top: Villa.
Bottom: Stepstones.
Right: Waterscape at the reception.

Information Center Nolte-Küchen

Löhne, Germany
Landscape Design: Nagel Landschaftsarchitekten BDLA
Completion: 2005
Client: Nolte-Küchen
Photos: Nagel Landschaftsarchitekten BDLA

The Nolte-Küchen Company is a kitchen manufacturer based in the center of Löhne in Westphalia. A central forecourt – designed 2005 by Nagel Landschaftsarchitekten – lies at the heart of the structure. Generously proportioned stairs with illuminated steps lead to the entrance of the information and training center along a number of water fountains. Individually designed elements encourage gathering and the enjoyment of views over the terraced water basin, which reflects the façade and back-lit expanded-metal screens. Thus an individual exterior for the base of the kitchen firm was fashioned, which also creates identity.

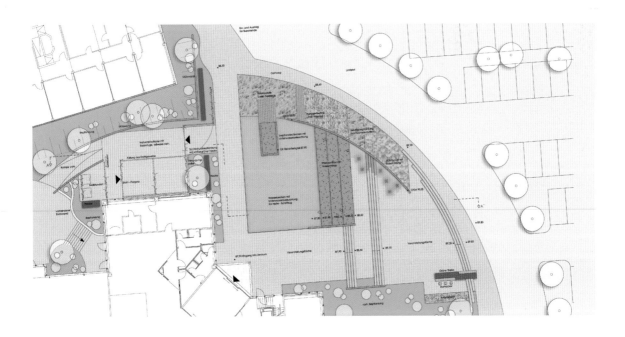

Left: Water fountain.
Right: Plan of garden layout.

Top: Night view.
Bottom: Waterwall.
Right: View from patio.

CYBER
Grill

Terminator 2: 3D and Aquazone Plaza

Los Angeles, CA, USA
Landscape Design: Rios Clementi Hale Studios
Architecture: Rios Clementi Hale Studios
Completion: 2000
Client: Universal Studios
Photos: Tom Bonner, Los Angeles

When Terminator 2: 3D proved to be the most popular attraction at Universal Studios' Florida theme park, Universal decided to add the attraction to the Hollywood site. The theater building carries a pattern of 'pixels' abstracted from the visuals used for the Terminator's computer screen visual field, and is punctuated by biomorphic curves of silver-gray: Cyberdyne's 'morphing liquid metal'. The adjoining Aquazone Plaza was developed as an outdoor alternative to a conventional 'feature' entertainment. It is centered around an elaborate interactive water feature, and provides resting and outdoor dining areas.

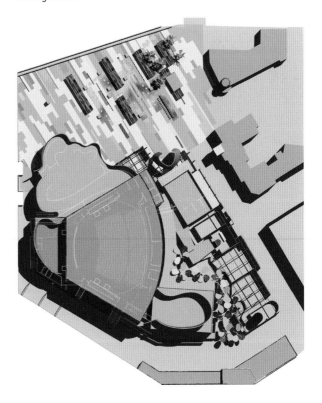

Left: Patrons traverse Aquazone to reach restaurants, retail and theater.
Right: Terminator 2: 3D and Aquazone Plaza site plan.

Top: Fictional headquarters building of the Cyberdyne Corporation of the Terminator movies provides a background.
Bottom: Lively plaza has interactive water features in front of retail, restaurants and theater.
Right: Aquazone Plaza sits in front of Terminator 2: 3D attraction at Universal Studios theme park.

Big Sky

Calgary, Alberta, Canada
Landscape Design: North Design Office
Completion: 2010
Client: Calgary Parks
Photos: Calgary Parks (136); Pete North NDO (138, 139)

Big Sky claims the central fountain space in Calgary's Olympic Plaza. Decorated with a pixelated sky graphic and a gathering of drifting birds, the fountain space is an attraction with or without water. The installation is designed to remind visitors of the unique vastness of Alberta's sky. A layer of bird models gently moves in response to the surrounding influences of light, wind and water. On their delicate stems, the birds are also reminiscent of the vast Prairie grasses. Depicting the dynamics of nature, the Big Sky installation connects the plaza to the vast and ephemeral qualities of the atmosphere.

Left: Detail of the birds.
Right: Perspective.

Top: Detail water.
Bottom: Overall view.
Right: Bird's-eye view.

Pampulha Ecological Park

Belo Horizonte, Brazil
Landscape Design: Gustavo Penna Arquiteto & Associados
Architecture: Gustavo Penna, Álvarro Hardy, Mariza
Machado Coelho
Completion: 2004
Client: Prefeitura Municipal de Belo Horizonte for SUDECAP -
Superintendência de Desenvolvimento da Capital
Photos: Jomar Bragança (140, 142), Eugênio Paccelli (143)

The object of this creation was to guarantee preservation and stability to the
area, island, peninsula and cove. Revitalizing these areas encourages the
community to take part in educational leisure activities as well as enabling
the zoological and botanical foundation to carry out science projects, environmental education and events. The park consists of five individual areas
– esplanade, reforested area, marsh, nature reserve and cove –, and mainly
focuses on the observation of the natural reserve. The adopted guidelines
are orientated to preserve the woodlands and its species in various different
ecosystems, incorporating trails for nature watching.

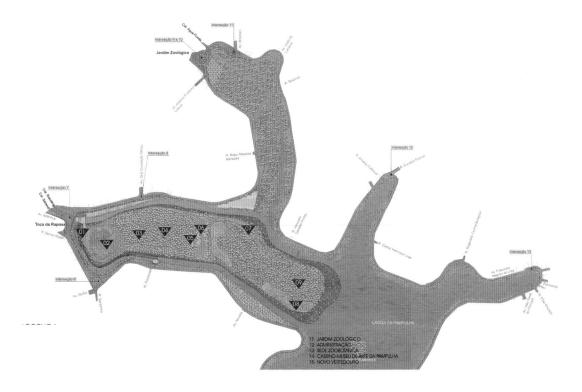

Left: View across the water.
Right: Site plan.

Top: Lawn and lake.
Bottom: Path and shelter.
Right: Bird's-eye view.

Cool Contemporary Classic

London, United Kingdom
Landscape Design: Charlotte Rowe Garden Design
Completion: 2006
Client: Private
Photos: Charlotte Rowe Garden Design/Light IQ

This long, narrow town garden is paved in pale cream limestone, inset with two cedar-decked pontoons bridging the 10-meter-long water rill, which runs down the length of the garden. The pontoons push the side boundaries out and help break up the space up to give the illusion of more space. Cedar benches and trellis unite the whole area and glass screens further divide the space. A row of pleached Carpinus Betulus runs along the end boundary wall, helping to screen the gardens beyond, and providing more privacy. Three multi stemmed Amelenchior Larmarkii growing among the paving and the pontoons, provide color in spring and fall. The lush, mixed evergreen and perennial planting with signature plants is carefully lit at night.

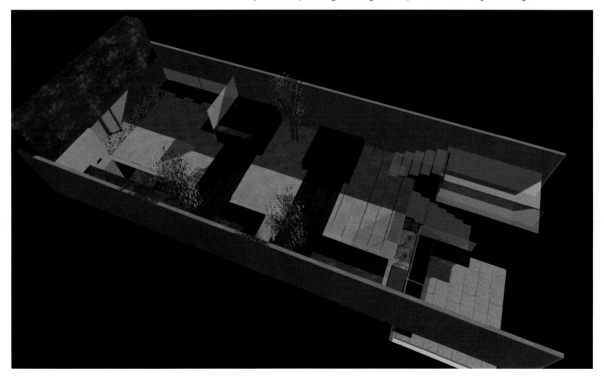

Left: Ten meter long water rill with two water chutes.
Right: Computer generated image.

Top: Water rill lit at night.
Bottom: View back to the house at night.
Right: View across the water rill from first floor balcony.

146

Aramsa Garden Spa

Singapore, Singapore
Landscape Design: Formwerkz Architects
Architecture: Formwerkz Architects
Completion: 2006
Client: Garden Spas Pte
Photos: Maurice Color Box

This garden spa is conceptualized as an extension of the park it occupies. Diagrammatically, a network of curves is superimposed over a grid of existing structures, slicing the compound into distinct zones and acting as a programmatic and circulation device. The landscape and gardens serve as optical frames and additionally function as privacy screens. As one circulates through the space, one constantly views gardens in the foreground while slivers of openings and lattices in the curved walls suggest other interspersed gardens in the background and the private strata beyond. The gardens unify the whole area and simultaneously separate the different units from each other.

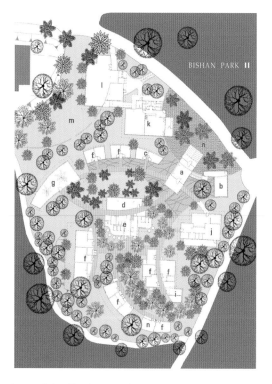

Left: Network of curved linkways that weaved between the various pockets of landscape gardens.
Right: Site plan.

149

Top: Strategic openings for access as well as framed views.
Bottom: Night view of the main landscaped court, with the silhouette of the cattails cast on the sweeping curve wall.
Right: View of spa retail approach from the reception via a pond.

Minato-Mirai Business Square

Yokohama, Japan
Landscape Design: Earthscape
Completion: 2004
Client: Tokyo-Kaijyokasai
Photos: Shigeki Asanuma

Yokohama grew up with the sea. These days, it is developing toward the sky by the construction of high-rise buildings on land. This land art construction symbolizes a pond and exists on the boundary between the sea and the sky. On the pond, words relating to the sky will appear and then disappear, reflected in the water's mirror surface. The words relating to the sea will appear from the bottom after the water has gone. In this way people can rethink their own existence by reminding themselves of their origins. The people were born from the sea and grew up on the land.

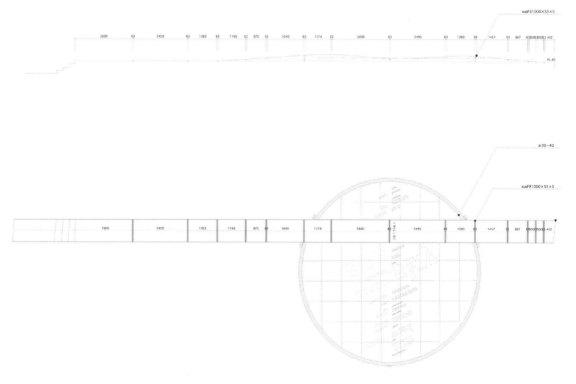

Left: Bassin.
Right: Section and floor plan.

Top: Path leading through bassin.
Bottom: Writings under water.
Right: Footprints on path leading upstairs.

Henry C. Beck Jr. Park

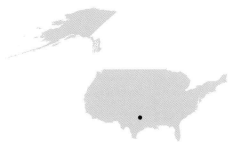

Dallas, TX, USA
Landscape Design: MESA
Architecture: Beck Group
Completion: 2004
Client: Beck Group
Photos: Tom Jenkins, Dallas

Beck Park, located near the Dallas Museum of Art and Nasher Sculpture Center, was built to celebrate the life of Henry C. Beck, Jr., founder of Beck Construction. This award-winning park provides exquisite detailing and museum quality work. Each of the several outdoor rooms offers a different focus and experience. A shady grove of trees with tables and chairs for outdoor lunch breaks is the largest room; the smallest is quiet and contemplative. This project is an outstanding example of quality open space in an urban environment and serves as a catalyst for new restaurants and retail space.

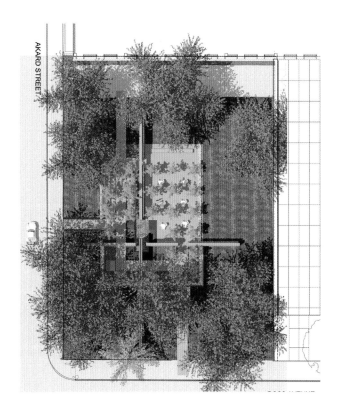

Left: View from south-east.
Right: Plan of plant arrangement.

Top: View of Beck Park from Ross Street.
Bottom: Beck Park at night.
Right: Evening image of Pennsylvania bluestone.

Hong Luo Club

Beijing, China
Landscape Design: MAD architects
Architecture: MAD architects
Completion: 2006
Client: Beijing Earth Real Estate Development Company
Photos: MAD

The expansion of Beijing city has intensively accelerated the development of its periphery areas over the last few years. This has aided the development of the first space typology in China. A wooden bridge was introduced as an access to the Club House. The house has two areas, one is a swimming pool floating on the lake, the other is an underwater platform. Two major roads converge at the center of the house and reach all the way up, along an ascending roof. The main access will bring the visitor to under the water level, giving visitors the feeling that they are actually walking in the lake. The outdoor swimming pool is built into the lake, which keeps the surfaces at the same level.

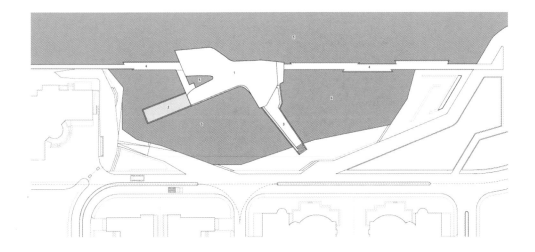

Left: Main access facing the banks.
Right: Site plan.

Top: Main access towards house.
Bottom: Perspective of the house with its two bridges.
Right: Side view at twilight.

Fairview Estate

Paarl, Western Cape, South Africa
Landscape Design: Tanya de Villiers of CNdV Africa
Completion: ongoing
Client: Charles Back of Fairview Estate
Photos: Christof Heierli

Fairview Estate is an ongoing landscape project. Unique to this project is the fact that most of the construction work was carried out by farm workers, supervised by the landscape architect. In 2000, the client wanted to transform the old farm into a venue for wine and cheese tasting. The farm road was re-routed and retaining walls were built to achieve a level garden space as a romantic setting for the historic buildings. Traditional forms and styles were used for the detailing of the walls and choice of materials, while the selected plants reflect the eras from which the buildings date. The goat tower, a focal point, is an icon of the cheese dairy. Recently the 'Goatshed' restaurant was added to the tranquil setting of the Cape 'werf' garden.

Left: The central traditional pond cools the garden during hot summers.
Right: Plan of garden layout.

Top: Upper garden space.
Bottom: Traditional materials.
Right: Walls with developed patina.

Parque del Agua

Bucaramanga, Colombia
Architects: Lorenzo Castro J., Juan Camilo Santamaría D., Sergio Garcia C.
Completion: 2004
Client: Acueducto de Bucaramanga
Photos: Felipe Uribe (168), Guillermo Quintero (170 a., 171), Lorenzo Castro (170 b.)

Formerly a water processing plant, "Morrorrico" was a center of attraction in Bucaramanga from the 1930s until it was shut in 2002. After making the decision to close the plant down, the Water Supply Company decided to turn it into an open, public garden for the city. The project creates a new natural setting that includes the existing elements: vegetation, topography, hydraulic infrastructure, the old plant's buildings and the new buildings of the company's headquarters. The new geometry accompanies these elements, and gradually adapts to the ground, modifying the area while being modified at the same time. The area appears altered and softened in its surface by the subtle topography, the water paths, the walkways and the exuberant vegetation.

Left: Cascading water.
Right: Layers of the intervention.

Top: Reflecting pools and parks fencing.
Bottom: Timber deck and waterwall at night.
Right: Main path and water.

Index

Creatives

Places

Jacob Isaacksz. van Ruisdael: Mill at Wijk at Duurstede, 1670.